From Ronnie / Sept '4

POEMS

by

ALLAN RAMSAY

POEMS

Epistles,
Fables,
Satires,
Elegies
&
Lyrics

by

ALLAN RAMSAY.

From the Edition printed by Thomas Ruddiman
for the Author. Edinburgh, 1721-1728.

Edited by
H. HARVEY WOOD
and published for
THE SALTIRE SOCIETY
by
OLIVER AND BOYD LTD.
1940.

PRINTED IN GREAT BRITAIN BY
OLIVER AND BOYD LTD., EDINBURGH

CONTENTS

	PAGE
The Poet's Wish : An Ode	9
The Conclusion	10
1726. Verses on the Last Leaf of the Bannatyne Manuscript in the Advocates' Library	12
To the Ph—. An Ode	13
To the Whin-Bush Club, The Bill of Allan Ramsay	15
To Mr. William Starrat	16
Lines from an Epistle to James Clerk, Esq., of Pennycuick	18
Familiar Epistles between Lieutenant William Hamilton and Allan Ramsay	20
An Epistle to Mr. James Arbuckle of Belfast, A.M.	25
Epistle to the Honourable Duncan Forbes, Lord Advocate	30
The Twa Books	32
The Chamaeleon	34
The Ape and the Leopard	35
The Twa Cats and the Cheese	37
Elegy on Lucky Wood in the Canongate, May 1717	38
Elegy on John Cowper Kirk-Treasurer's Man, *Anno* 1714	42
Elegy on Maggy Johnston, who died *Anno* 1711	46
Lucky Spence's Last Advice	50
My Peggy is a Young Thing	54
This is no My Ain House	55
The Carle He Came O'er the Croft	56
O Mither Dear ! I 'Gin to Fear	57
Up in the Air	58
The Widow	59
Nanny O	60
The Lass of Peattie's Mill	61
Bessy Bell and Mary Gray	62
For the Sake of Somebody	63
Ann Thou Were My Ain Thing	64
Glossary	66

INTRODUCTION

ALLAN RAMSAY was born on October 15, 1684 or 1685, in Leadhills, Lanarkshire. While he was yet an infant, his mother, recently widowed, married again ; and, about the year 1700, Ramsay left Leadhills for Edinburgh, where he became, first an apprentice, and later a master wigmaker. By 1710, he was a burgess ; by 1716 a constable, and by 1718 a lieutenant in the Train Bands. About 1724, he quitted the trade of wigmaking for that of bookselling, in which he had, since 1718, been interested. Before 1728, Ramsay started a circulating library in Edinburgh, perhaps the first venture of the kind in Britain ; and in 1729 he and his son, Allan Ramsay the painter, were among the twenty-eight foundation or charter members of the Academy of St Luke, "for the encouragement of the excellent arts of Painting, Sculpture, Architecture, etc."—over forty years earlier than the foundation of the English Royal Academy. As a bookseller, pamphleteer and adapter, Ramsay had long been interested in the stage, and in November, 1736, he opened the New Theatre in Carrubber's Close, Edinburgh's first regular theatre. There was furious opposition from the first, and his opponents, using the Licensing Act of 1737 as a stalking-horse, wrecked the venture, involving Ramsay, apparently, in considerable loss. Ramsay's various premises as bookseller and librarian were, according to credible tradition, meeting-places for the best and wittiest of Edinburgh society, and into the active club-life of early eighteenth century Edinburgh the poet seems to have entered with more than usual gusto. Many of these clubs were centres of Jacobite sentiment, but the Jacobitism of Ramsay was tempered by common-sense and discretion. He was a patriot in a larger sense ; and though he was out in neither the '15 nor the '45, he could justly claim (as he did claim in his address " To his Grace John Duke of Roxburgh ") to have rendered national service as a Scots Poet. Indeed it may be doubted if any Scotsman ever served the best interests of his country more faithfully, more intelligently, or more happily than Allan Ramsay.

To most Scotsmen to-day he is known as the author of *The Gentle Shepherd*. I hope it may be possible in the near future to reprint that charming pastoral comedy in its entirety : the present volume is concerned with his shorter poems—epistles, fables, satires, comic poems and lyrics.

This does not pretend to be a complete or a comparative text. I understand that the Scottish Text Society has in preparation a full edition, at the hands of Professor Burns Martin [from whose life of the poet the above outline is derived] and Dr. J. W. Oliver. This text merely reprints from the Ruddiman two-volume edition of 1721-28 (referred to throughout as " 1728 ") with reference, where necessary, to the edition of 1800. The only notes for which space could be found in this reprint are the notes given in Ruddiman's edition. They are almost an essential part of the text.

Readers who wish to know more about Ramsay are referred to Burns Martin's *Allan Ramsay, A Study of his Life and Works* (Harvard University Press, 1931) and Andrew Gibson's *New Light on Allan Ramsay*, Edinburgh and Belfast, 1927. Oliphant Smeaton's *Allan Ramsay*, in the Famous Scots Series, Edinburgh and London, 1896, may be read as a work of imagination. It is full of unsupported statements, wild inventions, and palpable forgeries.

H. H. W.

THE POET'S WISH: AN ODE.

Quid dedicatum poscit Apollinem
Vates ?—Hor.

Frae great *Apollo*, Poet say,
What is thy Wish, what wadst thou hae,
    When thou bows at his Shrine ?
Not *Karss* o' *Gowrie's* * fertile Field,
Nor a' the Flocks the *Grampians* yield,
    That are baith sleek and fine :
Not costly Things brought frae afar,
    As Ivory, Pearl and Gems ;
Nor those fair Straths that water'd are
    With *Tay* and *Tweed's* smooth Streams,
        Which gentily and daintily
           Eat [1] down the flowry Braes,
        As greatly and quately [2]
           They wimple to the Seas.

Whaever by his kanny Fate
Is Master of a good Estate,
    That can ilk Thing afford,
Let him enjoy't withoutten Care,
And with the Wale of curious Fare
    Cover his ample Board.
Much dawted by the Gods is he,
    Wha to the *Indian* Plain,
Successfu' ploughs the wally Sea,
    And safe returns again,

---

* A large and fertile Plain on the *Tay*, in the Shire of *Perth*.

---

[1] 1800 Pare   [2] 1728 quietly

With Riches that hitches
　　Him high aboon the rest
Of sma' Fowk, and a' Fowk
　　That are wi' Poortith prest.

For me I can be well content
To eat my Bannock on the Bent,
　　And kitchen't wi' fresh Air ;
Of Lang-kail I can make a Feast,
And cantily had up my Crest,
　　And laugh at Dishes rare.
Nought frae *Apollo* I demand,
　　But throw a lengthen'd Life
My outer Fabrick firm may stand,
　　And Saul clear without Strife.
　　　　May he then but gie then
　　　　　　Those Blessings for my Skair,
　　　　I'll fairly and squairly
　　　　　　Quite a' and seek nae mair.

THE
CONCLUSION.

After the Manner of Horace, ad librum suum.

Dear vent'rous Book, e'en take thy Will,
And scowp around the Warld thy fill :
Wow ! ye're newfangle to be seen,
In guilded Turky clade, and clean.
Daft giddy Thing ! to dare thy Fate,
And spang o'er Dikes that scar the blate :
But mind when anes ye're to the Bent,
(Altho in vain) ye may repent.
Alake, I'm flied thou aften meet,
A Gang that will thee sourly treat,

And ca' thee dull for a' thy Pains,
When Damps distress their drouzie Brains.
I dinna doubt whilst thou art new,
Thou'lt Favour find frae not a few,
But when thou'rt rufl'd and forfairn,
Sair thumb'd by ilka Coof or Bairn ;
Then, then by Age ye may grow wise,
And ken things common gies nae Price.
I'd fret, wae's me ! to see the lye
Beneath the Bottom of a Pye,
Or cow'd out Page by Page to wrap
Up Snuff, or Sweeties in a Shap.

AWAY sic Fears, gae spread my Fame,
And fix me an immortal Name ;
Ages to come shall thee revive,
And gar thee with new Honours live.
The future Criticks I forsee
Shall have their Notes on Notes on thee :
The Wits unborn shall Beauties find
That never enter'd in my Mind.

Now when thou tells how I was bred,
But hough enough * to a mean Trade ;
To ballance that, pray let them ken
My Saul to higher Pitch cou'd sten :
And when ye shaw I'm scarce of Gear,
Gar a' my Virtues shine mair clear.
Tell, I the best and fairest please,
A little Man that loo's my Ease,
And never thole these Passions lang
That rudely mint to do me wrang.

GIN ony want to ken my Age,
See *Anno Dom.* on Title Page ;

* Very indifferently.

This Year when Springs by Care and Skill
The spacious † leaden Conduits fill,
And first flow'd up the *Castle-hill*.
When South-Sea Projects cease to thrive,
And only *North-Sea* seems alive,
Tell them your Author's Thirty five.

† The new Lead Pipes for conveying Water to *Edinburgh*, of $4\frac{1}{2}$ Inches Diameter within, and $\frac{6}{10}$ of an Inch in thickness ; all cast in a Mould invented by the ingenious Mr. *Harding* of *London*.

1726

VERSES

ON THE LAST LEAF OF THE BANNATYNE MANUSCRIPT IN THE ADVOCATES' LIBRARY.

In seventeen hundred twenty-four,
    Did Allan Ramsay keen-
ly gather from this book that store,
    Which fills his Evergreen.

Thrice fifty and sax towmonds neat,
    Frae when it was collected ;
Let worthy poets hope good fate,
    Thro' time they'll be respected.

Fashion of words and wit may change,
    And rob in part their fame,
And make them to dull fops look strange,
    But sense is still the same ;

And will bleez bright to that clear mind,
    That loves the ancient strains,
Like good Carmichael, patron kind,
    To whom this book pertains.

FINIS *quod ALLAN RAMSAY.*

[Reprinted from the edition of 1800.]

TO THE PH——. AN ODE.

Vides ut alta stet nive candidum
Soracte.—HORACE.

LOOK up to *Pentland*'s towring Tap,[1]
Buried beneath great Wreaths of Snaw,
O'er ilka Cleugh, ilk Scar and Slap,
As high as ony *Roman* Wa'.

DRIVING their Baws frae Whins or Tee,
There's no ae [2] Gowfer to be seen,
Nor dousser Fowk wysing a Jee
The Byass [3] Bouls on *Tamson*'s Green.

THEN fling on Coals, and ripe the Ribs,
And beek the House baith Butt and Ben,
That Mutchken Stoup it hads but Dribs,
Then let's get in the tappit Hen.

GOOD Claret best keeps out the Cauld,
And drives away the Winter soon,
It makes a Man baith gash and bauld,
And heaves his Saul beyond the Moon.

LEAVE to the Gods your ilka Care,
If that they think us worth their While,
They can a Rowth of Blessings spare,
Which will our fashious Fears beguile.

FOR what they have a Mind to do,
That will they do, should we gang wood,
If they command the Storms to blaw,
Then upo' sight the Hailstains thud.

---

[1] 1728 Taps,   [2] 1800 nae   [3] 1800 byast

A 2

But soon as e'er they cry, Be quate,[1]
The blatt'ring Winds dare nae mair move,
But cour into their Caves, and wait
The high Command of supreme *Jove*.

Let neist Day come as it thinks fit,
The present Minute's only ours,
On Pleasure let's imploy our Wit,
And laugh at Fortune's feckless Power.

Be sure ye dinna quat the Grip
Of ilka Joy when ye are young,
Before auld Age your Vitals nip,
And lay ye twafald o'er a Rung.

Sweet Youth's a blyth and heartsome Time,
Then Lads and Lasses while it's *May*,
Gae pou the Gowan in its Prime,
Before it wither and decay.

Watch the saft Minutes of Delyte,
When *Jenny* speaks beneath her Breath,
And kisses, laying a the Wyte
On you if she kepp ony Skaith.

Haith ye're ill bred, she'll smiling say,
Ye'll worry me ye greedy Rook ;
Syne frae your Arms she'll rin away,
And hide her sell in some dark Nook :

Her Laugh will lead you to the Place
Where lies the Happiness ye want,
And plainly tells you to your Face,
Nineteen Nay-says are haff a Grant.

---

[1] 1728 Bequiet,   1800 " Be quiet,"

Now to her heaving Bosom cling,
And sweetly toolie for a Kiss,
Frae her fair Finger whop a Ring,
As Taiken of a Future Bliss.

THESE Bennisons, I'm very sure,
Are of the Gods indulgent Grant ;
Then surly Carles,[1] whisht, forbear
To plague us with your whining Cant.

[1] *Quy.* " Carlies," see p. 27, l. 24.

TO THE

WHIN-BUSH CLUB,*

THE BILL

Of *ALLAN RAMSAY*.

OF *Crawfurd-Moor*, born in *Leadhill*,†
Where Min'ral Springs *Glengoner* ‡ fill,
    Which joins sweet flowing *Clyde*,
Between auld *Crawfurd-Lindsay's* Towers,
And where *Deneetne* rapid pours
    His Stream thro' *Glotta's* Tide ;
Native of *Clydsdale's* upper Ward,
    Bred Fifteen Summers there,

* This Club consists of *Clydsdale*-Shire Gentlemen, who frequently
meet at a diverting Hour, and keep up a good Understanding amongst
themselves over a friendly Botle.   And from a charitable Principle,
easily collect into their Treasurer's Box a small Fond, which has many
a Time relieved the Distresses of indigent Persons of that Shire.

    † In the Parish of *Crawfurd-Moor*, famous for the Lead and Gold
Mines belonging to the Earl of *Hoptoun*.

    ‡ The Name of a small River, which takes its Rise from the *Lead-hills*,
and enters *Clyde* between the Castle of *Crawfurd* and the mouth of
Deneetne, another of the Branches of *Clyde*.

Tho, to my Loss I'm no a Laird
By Birth, my Title's fair
To bend wi' ye and spend wi' ye
An Evening, and gaffaw,
If Merit and Spirit
Be found without a Flaw.

SINCE dously ye do nought at Random,
Then take my Bill to *Avisandum* ;
And if there's nae Objection,
I'll deem't my Honour and be glad
To come beneath your *Whin-Bush* Shade,
And claim to its [1] Protection.
If frae the Caverns of a Head
That's boss, a Storm should blaw,
Etling wi' Spite to rive my Reed,
And give my Muse a Fa',
When poring and soaring
O'er *Heleconian* Heights,
She traces these Places
Where *Cynthius* delights.

[1] 1800 from it

TO MR. WILLIAM STARRAT
*on receiving the above Epistle.**

FRAE fertile Fields, where nae curs'd Ethers creep,
To stang the Herds that in Rash-busses sleep ;
Frae where Saint *Patrick*'s Blessing freed the Bogs
Frae Taids, and Asks, and ugly creeping Frogs ;
Welcome to me's the Sound of *STARRAT*'s Pipe,
Welcome, as Westlen Winds, or Berries ripe,
When speeling up the Hill, the *Dog-days* Heat
Gars a young thirsty Shepherd pant and sweat :
Thus while I climb the Muses Mount with Care,
Sic friendly Praises give refreshing Air.

* See *Epistle from Mr. William Starrat*, ed. 1728, II, 106-109.

O ! may the Lasses loo thee for thy Pains,
And may thou lang breathe healsome o'er the Plains :
Lang mayst thou teach, with round and nooked Lines,
Substantial Skill, that's worth rich Siller Mines ;
To shaw how Wheels can gang with greatest Ease,
And what Kind Barks sails smoothest o'er the Seas ;
How Wind-mills shou'd be made,—and how they work
The Thumper that tells Hours upon the Kirk :
How Wedges rive the Aik :—How Pullieses
Can lift on highest Roofs the greatest Trees ;
Rug frae its Roots the Craig of *Edinburgh* Castle,
As easily as I cou'd break my Whistle.—
What Pleughs fits a wet Soil, and whilk the dry ;
And mony a thousand useful Things forby.

I own 'tis cauld Encouragement to sing,
When round ane's Lugs the blatran Hailstanes ring ;
But feckfu' Folk can front the bauldest Wind,
And slonk thro' Moors, and never fash their Mind.
Aft have I wid throu' Glens with chorking Feet,
When neither Plaid nor Kelt cou'd fend the Weet ;
Yet blythly wald I bang out o'er the Brae, ⎫
And stend o'er Burns as light as ony Rae, ⎬
Hoping the Morn might prove a better Day. ⎭
Then let's to Lairds and Ladies leave the Spleen,
While we can dance and whistle o'er the Green.
Mankind's Account of Good and Ill's a Jest,
Fancy's the Rudder, and Content's a Feast.

DEAR Friend of mine, ye but o'er meikle roose
The lawly Mints of my poor moorland Muse,
Wha looks but blate, when even'd to either twa,
That lull'd the Deel, or bigg'd the *Theban* Wa' ;
But trowth 'tis natural for us a' to wink
At our ain Fauts, and Praises frankly drink :
Fair fa' ye then, and may your Flocks grow rife,
And may nae Elf twin *Crummy* of her Life.

THE Sun shines sweetly, a' the Lift looks blue,
O'er Glens hing hovering Clouds of rising Dew ;
Maggy the bonniest Lass of a' our Town,
Brent is her Brow, her Hair a curly brown,
I have a Tryst with her, and maun away,
Then ye'll excuse me till anither Day,
When I've mair Time ; for shortly I'm to sing
Some dainty Sangs, that sall round *Crochan* ring.

Lines from

AN EPISTLE TO JAMES CLERK, ESQ. OF PENNYCUICK.

[From the ed. of 1800]

. . . But here, dear Sir, do not mistake me,
As if grace did sae far forsake me,
As to allege that all poor fellows,
Unblest with wealth, deserv'd the gallows.
Na, God forbid that I should spell
Sae vile a fortune to mysell,
Tho' born to not ae inch of ground,
I keep my conscience white and sound ;
And tho' I ne'er was a rich heaper,
To make that up I live the cheaper ;
By this ae knack I've made a shift
To drive ambitious care a-drift ;
And now in years and sense grown auld,
In ease I like my limbs to fauld.
Debts I abhor, and plan to be
Frae shochling trade and danger free,
That I may, loos'd frae care and strife,
With calmness view the edge of life ;
And when a full ripe age shall crave,
Slide easily into my grave.

Now seventy years are o'er my head,
And thirty mae may lay me dead ;
Should dreary care then stunt my muse,
And gar me aft her jogg refuse ?
Sir, I have sung, and yet may sing,
Sonnets that o'er the dales may ring,
And in gash glee couch moral saw,
Reese virtue and keep vice in awe ;
Make villainy look black and blue,
And give distinguish'd worth its due ;
Fix its immortal fame in verse,
That men till doomsday shall rehearse.

I have it even within my pow'r,
The very kirk itself to scow'r,
And that you'll say's a brag right bauld ;
But did not Lindsay this of auld ?
Sir David's satyres help'd our nation
To carry on the Reformation,
And gave the scarlet whore a box
Mair snell than all the pelts of Knox.

Thus far, Sir, with no mean design,
To you I've poured out my mind,
And sketch'd you forth the toil and pain
Of them that have their bread to gain
With cares laborious, that you may,
In your blest sphere be ever gay,
Enjoying life with all that spirit
That your good sense and virtues merit.
Adieu, and ma'ye as happy be
As ever shall be wish'd by me,

> Your ever obliged,
> humble servant,
> ALLAN RAMSAY.

PENNYCUICK,
May 9, 1755.

FAMILIAR EPISTLES

BETWEEN

Lieutenant *William Hamilton* and *Allan Ramsay*.

EPISTLE I.

Gilbertfield June 26th, 1719.

O Fam'd and celebrated ALLAN !
Renowned RAMSAY, canty Callan,
There's nowther Highlandman nor Lawlan,
    In Poetrie,
But may as soon ding down *Tamtallan* *
    As match wi' thee.

FOR ten Times ten, and that's a hunder,
I ha'e been made to gaze and wonder,
When frae *Parnassus* thou didst thunder,
    Wi' Wit and Skill,
Wherefore I'll soberly knock under,
    And quat my Quill.

OF Poetry the hail Quintessence
Thou has suck'd up, left nae Excrescence
To petty Poets, or sic Messens,
    Tho round thy Stool,
They may pick Crumbs, and lear some Lessons
    At *Ramsay*'s School.

THO *Ben* † and *Dryden* of Renown
Were yet alive in *London* Town,
Like Kings contending for a Crown ;
    'Twad be a Pingle,
Whilk o' you three wad gar Words sound
    And best to gingle.

* An old Fortification upon the Firth of *Forth* in *East Lothian.*
† The [1728 misprints " Tho "] celebrated *Ben Johnston.*

TRANSFORM'D may I be to a Rat,
Wer't in my Pow'r but I'd create
Thee upo' sight the Laureat ‡
          Of this our Age,
Since thou may'st fairly claim to that
          As thy just Wage.

LET modern Poets bear the Blame,
Gin they respect not *Ramsay*'s Name,
Wha soon can gar them greet for Shame,
          To their great Loss ;
And send them a' right sneaking hame
          Be Weeping-Cross.

WHA bourds wi' thee had need be warry,
And lear wi' Skill thy Thrust to parry,
When thou consults thy Dictionary
          Of ancient Words,
Which come from thy Poetick Quarry,
          As sharp as Swords.

Now tho I should baith reel and rottle,
And be as light as *Aristotle*,
At *Ed'nburgh* we sall ha'e a Bottle
          Of reaming Claret,
Gin that my haff-pay § Siller Shottle
          Can safely spare it.

‡ *Scots* Ramsay *press'd hard, and sturdily vaunted,*
  He'd fight for the Laurel before he would want it :
  But risit Apollo, *and cry'd, Peace there old Stile,*
  Your Wit is obscure to one half of the Isle.

                              B. Sess. of Poets.

§ He held his Commission honourably in my Lord *Hyndford*'s
Regiment.
                    And may the Stars wha shine aboon
                    With Honour notice real Merit,
                    Be to my Friend auspicious soon,
                    And cherish ay sae fine a Spirit.

At Crambo then we'll rack our Brain,
Drown ilk dull Care and aiking Pain,
Whilk aften does our Spirits drain
       Of true Content ;
Wow, Wow ! but we's be wonder fain,
       When thus acquaint.

Wi' Wine we'll gargarize our Craig,
Then enter in a lasting League,
Free of Ill Aspect or Intrigue,
       And gin you please it,
Like Princes when met at the *Hague*,
       We'll solemnize it.

Accept of this and look upon it
With Favour, tho poor I have done it ;
Sae I conclude and end my Sonnet,
       Who am most fully,
While I do wear a Hat or Bonnet,
       Yours,—wanton *Willy*.

Postscript.

By this my Postscript I incline
To let you ken my hail Design
Of sic a lang imperfect Line,
       Lyes in this Sentence,
To cultivate my dull Ingine
       By your Acquaintance.

Your Answer therefore I expect,
And to your Friend you may direct,
At *Gilbertfield* * do not neglect
       When ye have Leisure,
Which I'll embrace with great Respect
       And perfect Pleasure.

       * Nigh *Glasgow.*

ANSWER I.

Edinburgh, July 10th, 1719.

Sonse fa me, witty, wanton *Willy*,
Gin blyth I was na as a Filly ;
Not a fow Pint, nor short Hought Gilly,
  Or Wine that's better,
Cou'd please sae meikle, my dear Billy,
  As thy kind Letter.

Before a Lord and eik a Knight,
In Gossy *Don*'s be Candle Light,
There first I saw't, and ca'd it right,
  And the maist feck
Wha's seen 't sinsyne, they ca'd as tight
  As that on *Heck*.

Ha, heh ! thought I, I canna say
But I may cock my Nose the Day,
When *Hamilton* the bauld and gay
  Lends me a Heezy,
In Verse that slides sae smooth away,
  Well tell'd and easy.

Sae roos'd by ane of well kend Mettle,
Nae sma did my Ambition pettle
My canker'd Criticks it will nettle,
  And e'en sae be't :
This Month I'm sure I winna settle,
  Sae proud I'm wi't.

When I begoud first to cun Verse,
And cou'd your *Ardry Whins* rehearse,
Where *Bonny Heck* * ran fast and fierce,
  It warm'd my Breast ;
Then Emulation did me pierce,
  Whilk since ne'er ceast.

* The last Words of *Bonny Heck*, of which he was Author.

MAY I be licket wi' a Bittle,
Gin of your Numbers I think little ;
Ye're never rugget, shan, nor kittle,
        But blyth and gabby,
And hit the Spirit to a Title,
        Of Standart *Habby*.†

YE'LL quat your Quill !   That were ill-willy,
Ye's sing some mair yet, nill ye will ye,
O'er meikle Haining wad but spill ye,
        And gar ye sour,
Then up and war them a' yet, *Willy*,
        'Tis in your Power.

To knit up Dollers in a Clout,
And then to eard them round about,
Syne to tell up, they downa lout
        To lift the Gear ;
The Malison lights on that Rout,
        Is plain and clear.

THE Chiels of *London*, *Cam*, and *Ox*,
Ha'e rais'd up great Poetick Stocks
Of *Rapes*, of *Buckets*, *Sarks* and *Locks*,
        While we neglect
To shaw their betters.   This provokes
        Me to reflect

ON the lear'd Days of *Gawn Dunkell*,‡
Our Country then a Tale cou'd tell,
Europe had nane mair snack and snell
        At Verse or Prose ;

† The Elegy on *Habby Simpson* Piper of *Kilbarchan*, a finish'd Piece
of its Kind.
‡ *Gawn Douglass* Brother to the Earl of *Angus* Bishop of *Dunkell*,
who besides several original Poems, hath left a most exact Translation
of *Virgil's Æneis*.

Out Kings § were Poets too themsell,
  Bauld and Jocose.

To *Ed'nburgh*, Sir, when e'er ye come,
I'll wait upon ye, there's my Thumb,
Were't frae the Gill-bells ‖ to the Drum,
  And take a Bout,
And faith I hope we'll no sit dumb,
  Nor yet cast out.

§ *James* the First and Fifth.
‖ From Half an Hour before Twelve at Noon, when the Musick
Bells begin to play, frequently called the Gill-bells, from Peoples
taking a wheting Dram at that Time. *To the Drum*, Ten a Clock at
Night, when the Drum goes round to warn sober Folks to call for a Bill.

AN

EPISTLE

TO

Mr. James Arbuckle *of* Belfast, A. M.

Edinburgh, January 1719.

As Errant Knight with Sword and Pistol,
Bestrides his Steed with mighty Fistle ;
Then stands some Time in jumbled Swither
To ride in this Road or that ither ;
At last spurs on, and disna care for
A how, a what Way, or a wherefore.

 Or like extemporary Quaker,
Wasting his Lungs, t'enlighten weaker
Lanthorns of Clay, where Light is wanting,
With formless Phrase, and formal Canting ;
While *Jacob Behmen's* Salt * does season,
And saves his Thought frae corrupt Reason,

* A Quaker, who wrote Volumes of unintelligible enthusiastick
Bombast.

B

Gowling aloud with Motions queerest,
Yerking these Words out which ly nearest.

Thus I (no longer to illustrate
With Similies, lest I should frustrate
Design *Laconick* of a Letter,
With Heap of Language and no Matter,)
Bang'd up my blyth auld-fashion'd Whistle,
To sowf ye o'er a short Epistle,
Without Rule, Compasses, or Charcoal,
Or serious Study in a dark Hole.
Three Times I ga'e the Muse a Rug,
Then bate my Nails and claw'd my Lug ;
Still heavy, at the last my Nose
I prim'd with an inspiring Dose,†
Then did Ideas dance, (dear safe us !)
As they'd been daft.—Here ends the Preface.

Good Mr. *James Arbuckle*, Sir,
(That's Merchant's Stile, as clean as Fir)
Ye're welcome back ‡ to *Caledonie*,
Lang Life and thriving light upon ye,
Harvest, Winter, Spring and Summer,
And ay keep up your heartsome Humor,
That ye may thro' your lucky Task go,
Of brushing up our Sister *Glasgow* ;
Where Lads are dextrous at improving,
And docile Lasses fair and loving :
But never tent these Fellows Girning,
Wha wear their Faces ay in Mourning,
And frae pure Dullness are malicious,
Terming ilk Turn that's witty, vicious.

Now, *Jamie*, in neist Place, *Secundo*,
To give you what's your Due in *mundo* ;

† *Vide* Mr. *Arbuckle*'s Poem on Snuff.
‡ Having been in his Native *Ireland* visiting his Friends.

That is to say in hame o'er Phrases,
To tell ye, Men of Mettle praises
Ilk Verse of yours when they can light on't,
And trouth I think they're in the right on't ;
For there's ay something sae auldfarran,
Sae slid, sae unconstrain'd and darrin,
In ilka Sample we have seen yet,
That little better e'er has been yet.
Sae much for that.—My Friend *Arbuckle*,
I ne'er afore roos'd ane sae muckle.
Fause Flat'ry nane but Fools will tickle,
That gars me hate it like auld *Nicol* :
But when ane's of his Merit conscious,
He's in the wrang, when prais'd, that glunshes.

THIRDLY, Not tether'd to Connection,
But rattling by inspir'd Direction,
When ever Fame, with Voice like Thunder,
Sets up a Chield a Warld's Wonder,
Either for slashing Fowk to dead,
Or having Wind-mills in his Head,
Or Poet, or an airy Beau,
Or ony twa Leg'd Rary-show,
They wha have never seen't are bissy
To speer what like a Carlie is he.

Imprimis then, for Tallness I
Am five Foot and four Inches high :
A Black-a-vic'd snod dapper Fallow,
Nor lean, nor overlaid wi' Tallow.
With Phiz of a *Morocco* Cut,
Resembling a late Man of Wit,
Auld-gabbet *Spec*,§ wha was sae Cunning
To be a Dummie ten Years running.

§ The Spectator, who gives us a fictitious Description of his short
Face and Taciturnity, that he had been esteem'd a dumb Man for ten
Years.

THEN for the Fabrick of my Mind,
'Tis mair to Mirth than Grief inclin'd.
I rather choose to laugh at Folly,
Than show Dislike by Melancholy ;
Well judging a sowr heavy Face
Is not the truest Mark of Grace.

I hate a Drunkard or a Glutton,
Yet am nae fae to Wine and Mutton.
Great Tables ne'er engag'd my Wishes,
When crowded with o'er mony Dishes,
A healthfu' Stomach sharply set
Prefers a Back-sey pipin het.

I never cou'd imagin't vicious
Of a fair Fame to be ambitious :
Proud to be thought a comick Poet, ⎫
And let a Judge of Numbers know it, ⎬
I court Occasion thus to show it. ⎭

SECOND of thirdly,—pray take heed,
Ye's get a short Swatch of my Creed.
To follow Method negatively
Ye ken takes Place of positively.
Well then, I'm nowther Whig nor Tory,
Nor Credit give to Purgatory.
Transub, *Loretta-house*, and mae Tricks,
As Prayers to Saints, *Katties* and *Patricks* ;
Nor *Asgilite*,‖ nor *Bess Clarksonian*,
Nor *Mountaineer*,¶ nor *Mugletonian* ;
Nor can believe, ant's nae great Ferly,
In *Cotmoor* Fowk,** and *Andrew Harley*.

‖ Mr. *Asgil*, a late Member of Parliament advanced (whether in
Jest or Earnest I know not) some very whimsical Opinions, particularly,
That People need not die if they pleas'd, but be translated alive to
Heaven like *Enoch* and *Elijah*. *Clerksonian*, *Bessy Clarkson* a *Lanerk*
Shire Woman. *Vide* the History of her Life and Principles.
¶ Our wild Folks, who always prefer a Hill-side to a Church under

Neist *Anti-Tolland*, *Blunt* and *Wh——*,[1]
Know positively I'm a Christian,
Believing Truths and thinking free,
Wishing thrawn Parties wad agree.

Say, wad ye ken my gate of Fending,
My Income, Management, and Spending?
Born to nae Lairdship, mair's the Pity!
Yet Denison of this fair City.
I make what honest Shift I can,
And in my ain House am Good-man,
Which stands on *Edinburgh's* Street the Sun-side,
I theek the out, and line the Inside
Of mony a douse and witty Pash,
And baith Ways gather in the Cash;
Thus heartily I graze and beau it,
And keep a Wife ay great wi' Poet.
Contented I have sic a Skair,
As does my Business to a Hair,
And fain wa'd prove to ilka *Scot*
That Poortith's no the Poet's Lot.

Fourthly and lastly baith togither,
Pray let us ken when ye come hither;
There's mony a canty Carle and me
Wa'd be much comforted to see ye.
But if your outward be Refractory,
Send us your inward Manufactory.
That when we're kedgy o'er our Claret,
We correspond may with your Spirit.

any civil Authority. *Mugletonian*, A kind of Quakers, so called from one *Mugleton*. See *Leslie's Snake in the Grass*.
** A Family or two who had a particular Religion of their own, valued themselves on using vain Repetitions in Prayers of 6 or 7 Hours long; were pleased with Ministers of no kind. *Andrew Harlaw* a dull Fellow of no Education was Head of the Party.

[1] 1800 Whiston,

ACCEPT of my kind Wishes, with
The same to Dons *Buttler* and *Smith* ;
Health Wit and Joy, Sauls large and free,
Be a' your Fates,—sae God be wi' ye.

EPISTLE

To the HONOURABLE

DUNCAN FORBES,

Lord Advocate.

SHUT in a Closet six Foot square,
No fash'd with meikle Wealth or Care,
    I pass the live lang Day ;
Yet some ambitious Thoughts I have,
Which will attend me to my Grave,
    Sic busked Baits they lay.

THESE keep my Fancy on the Wing,
Something that's blyth and snack to sing,
    And smooth the runkled Brow :
Thus Care I happily beguile,
Hoping a Plaudit and a Smile,
    Frae best of Men, like You.

YOU, wha in kittle Casts of State,
When Property demands Debate,
    Can right what is dung [1] wrang ;
Yet blythly can, when ye think fit,
Enjoy your Friend, and judge the Wit
    And Slidness of a Sang.

How mony, your Reverse, unblest,
Whase Minds gae wandring through a Mist,
    Proud as the Thief in Hell,

[1] 1800 done

Pretend, forsooth, they're gentle Fowk,
'Cause Chance gi'es them of Gear the Yowk,
 And better Cheils the Shell?

I've seen a We'an aft vex it sell,
And greet, because it was not tall:
 Heez'd on a Board, O than!
Rejoicing in the artfu' Height,
How smirky look'd the little Wight!
 And thought it sell a Man.

Sic Bairns are some blawn up a wee
With Splendor, Wealth and Quality,
 Upon these Stilts grown vain;
They o'er the Pows of poor Fowk stride,
And neither are to had nor bide,
 Thinking this Height their ain.

Now shou'd ane speer at sic a Puff,
What gars thee look sae big and bluff?
 Is't an attending Menzie?
Or fifty Dishes on your Table?
Or fifty Horses in your Stable?
 Or Heaps of glancing Cunzie?

Are these the things thou ca's thy sell?
Come, vain gigantick Shadow, tell,
 If thou sayest, Yes—I'll shaw
Thy Picture.—Mean's thy silly Mind,
Thy Wit's a croil, thy Judgment blind,
 And Love worth nought ava.

Accept our Praise, ye nobly born,
Whom Heaven takes Pleasure to adorn
 With ilka manly Gift;

In *Courts* or *Camps* to serve your Nation,
Warm'd with that generous Emulation
    Which your Forbears did lift.

In Duty, with Delight, to You
Th' inferior World [do] [1] justly bow,
    While You're the maist deny'd ;
Yet shall Your Worth be ever priz'd,
When struting Nathings are despis'd
    With a' their stinkan Pride.

This to set aff as I am able,
I'll frae a *Frenchman* thigg a Fable,
    And busk it in a Plaid :
And tho' it be a Bairn of * *Motte*'s,
When I have taught it to speak *Scots*,
    I am its second Dad.

* Mons. la Motte, who has written lately a curious Collection of Fables, from which the following is imitated.

---

[1] 1728 Th' inferior World justly bow,

THE TWA BOOKS *

Twa Books, near Neighbours in a Shop,
The tane a guilded *Turky* Fop,
The tither's Face was weather-beaten,
And Caf-skin Jacket sair worm-eaten.
The Corky, proud of his braw Suit,
Curl'd up his Nose, and thus cry'd out,
" Ah ! place me on some fresher Binks,
" Figh ! how this mouldy Creature stinks !
" How can a gentle Book like me
" Endure sic scoundrel Company ?

* Title supplied from 1800.

" What may Fowk say to see me cling
" Sae close to this auld ugly thing ;
" But that I'm of a simple Spirit,
" And disregard my proper Merit ? "

QUOTH Gray-baird, "*Whisht, Sir, with your Din,*
" *For a' your meritorious Skin,*
" *I doubt if you be worth within.*
" *For as auld-fashion'd as I look,*
" *May be I am the better Book.*

" O Heavens ! I canna thole the Clash
" Of this impertinent auld Hash ;
" I winna stay ae Moment langer."
" *My Lord, please to command your Anger ;*
" *Pray only let me tell you that——*"
" What wad this Insolent be at !
" Rot out your Tongue—Pray', Master *Symmer*,
" Remove me frae this dinsome *Rhimer :*
" If you regard your Reputation,
" And us of a distinguish'd Station,
" Hence frae this Beast let me be hurried,
" For with his Stour and Stink I'm worried."

SCARCE had he shook his paughty Crap,
When in a Customer did pap ;
He up douse *Stanza* lifts, and ey's him,
Turns o'er his Leaves, admires, and buys him :
This Book, said he, *is good and scarce,*
The Saul of Sense in sweetest Verse.
But reading Title of gilt cleathing,
Cries, *Gods ! wha buys this bonny naithing ?*
Nought duller e'er was put in Print :
Wow ! what a deal of Turky's tint !

Now, Sir, t'apply what we've invented,
You are the Buyer represented :

And, may your Servant hope
My Lays shall merit your Regard,
I'll thank the Gods for my Reward,
And smile at ilka Fop.

THE CHAMAELEON

Twa Travellers, as they were wa'king,
'Bout the *Chamaeleon* fell a ta'king,
(Sic think it shaws them mettl'd Men,
To say I've seen, and ought to ken ;)
Says ane, 'Tis a strange Beast indeed,
Four-footed, with a Fish's Head ;
A little Bowk, with a lang Tail,
And moves far slawer than a Snail ;
Of Colour like a Blawart blue ;—
Reply'd his Nibour, *That's no true ;*
For well I wat his Colour's Green,
If ane may true his ain twa Een ;
For I in Sun-shine saw him fair,
When he was dining on the Air.—
Excuse me, says the ither Blade,
I saw him better in the Shade,
And he is Blue.—*He's Green I'm sure.*—
Ye lied.—*And ye're the Son of a Whore.*—
Frae Words there had been Cuff and Kick,
Had not a Third come in the Nick,
Wha tenting them in this rough Mood,
Cry'd, Gentlemen, what ! are ye wood ?
What's ye'r Quarrel, and't may be speer't ?
Truth, says the tane, Sir, ye shall hear't :
The *Chamaeleon*, I say, he's Blue ;
He threaps he's Green.—Now, what say you ?
Ne'er fash ye'r sells about the Matter,
Says the sagacious Arbitrator,

He's Black.—Sae nane of you are right,
I view'd him well with Candle-light ;
And have it in my Pocket here,
Row'd in a Napkin hale and feer.
Fy ! said ae Cangler, *What d'ye mean ?*
I'll lay my Lugs on't, that he's Green.
Said th'ither, were I gawn to Death,
I'd swear he's Blue with my last Breath.
He's Black, the Judge maintain'd ay stout ;
And to convince them, whop'd him out :
But to Surprise of ane and a',
The *Animal* was White as Snaw,
And thus reprov'd them, " Shallow Boys,
" Away, away, make nae mair Noise ;
" Ye're a' three wrang, and a' three right,
" But learn to own your Nibours Sight
" As good as yours.—Your Judgment speak,
" But never be sae daftly weak
" T'imagine ithers will by Force
" Submit their Sentiments to yours ;
" As things in various Lights ye see,
" They'll ilka ane resemble me."

THE APE AND THE LEOPARD

THE *Ape* and *Leopard*, Beasts for Show,
The first a Wit, the last a Beau ;
To make a Penny at a Fair,
Advertis'd a' their Parts sae rare.
The tane gae out with meikle Wind,
His Beauty 'boon the brutal Kind ;
Said he, I'm kend baith far and near,
Even Kings are pleas'd when I appear :
And when I yield my vital Puff,
Queens of my Skin will make a Muff ;

My Fur sae delicate and fine,
With various Spots does sleekly shine.——

Now Lads and Lasses fast did rin
To see the Beast with bonny Skin :
His Keeper shaw'd him round about ;
They saw him soon, and soon came out.

But Master *Monky* with an Air
Hapt out, and thus harangu'd the Fair ;
Come, Gentlemen, and Ladies bonny,
I'll give ye Pastime for your Money :
I can perform, to raise your wonder,
Of pawky Tricks mae than a hunder.
My Cousin *Spottie*, true he's braw,
He has a curious Suit to shaw,
And nathing mair——But frae my Mind
Ye shall blyth Satisfaction find.
Sometimes I'll act a Cheil that's dull,
Look thoughtfu', grave, and wag my Scull ;
Then mimick a light-headed Rake,
When on a Tow my Houghs I shake :
Sometime, like modern Monks, I'll seem
To make a Speech, and nathing mean.
But come away, ye needna speer
What ye're to pay ; I'se no be dear :
And if we grudge for want of Sport,
I'll give it back t'ye at the Port.
The *Ape* succeeded, in Fowk went,—
Stay'd long,—and came out well content.
Sae much will Wit and Spirit please,
Beyond our Shape, and brawest Claiths.
How mony, ah ! of our fine Gallants
Are only *Leopards* * in their Talents !

* 1728 Leopard

THE TWA CATS AND THE CHEESE.

Twa *Cats* anes on a *Cheese* did light,
To which baith had an equal Right ;
But Disputes, sic as aft arise,
Fell out a sharing of the Prize.
Fair Play, said ane, ye bite o'er thick,
Thae Teeth of your's gang wonder quick :
Let's part it, else lang or the Moon
Be chang'd, the *Kebuck* will be done.
But wha's to do't ;—they're Parties baith,
And ane may do the other Skaith.
Sae with Consent away they trudge,
And laid the *Cheese* before a Judge :
A *Monkey* with a campsho Face,
Clerk to a Justice of the Peace,
A Judge he seem'd in Justice skill'd,
When he his Master's Chair [had] fill'd ;
Now Umpire chosen for Division,
Baith sware to stand by his Decision.
Demure he looks.—The *Cheese* he pales,—
He prives it good,—Ca's for the Scales ;
His Knife whops throw't,—in twa it fell ;
He puts ilk haff in either Shell :
Said he, We'll truly weigh the Case,
And strictest Justice shall have Place ;
Then lifting up the Scales, he fand
The tane bang up, the other stand :
Syne out he took the heaviest haff,
And ate a Knoost o't quickly aff,
And try'd it syne ;—it now prov'd light :
Friend Cats, said he, we'll do ye right.
Then to the ither haff he fell,
And laid till't teughly Tooth and Nail,
Till weigh'd again it lightest prov'd.
The Judge wha this sweet Process lov'd,

Still weigh'd the Case, and still ate on,
'Till Clients baith were weary grown,
And tenting how the Matter went,
Cry'd, Come, come, Sir, we're baith content.
Ye Fools, quoth he, and *Justice* too,
Maun be content as well as you.
Thus grumbled *they*, thus *he* went on,
Till baith the Haves were near hand done :
Poor *Pousies* now the Daffine saw
Of gawn for Nignyes to the Law ;
And bill'd the Judge, that he wad please
To give them the remaining Cheese :
To which his Worship grave reply'd,
The Dues of Court maun first be paid.
Now Justice pleas'd :—What's to the fore
Will but right scrimply clear your Score ;
That's our Decreet ;—gae hame and sleep,
And thank us ye're win aff sae cheap.

ELEGY

ON

Lucky *WOOD* in the *Canongate*,* *May* 1717.

O *Cannigate !* poor elritch Hole,
What Loss, what Crosses does thou thole !
London and Death † gars thee look drole,
        And hing thy Head ;
Wow, but thou has e'en a cauld Coal
        To blaw indeed.

* Lucky *Wood* kept an Ale-house in the *Canongate*, and was much
respected for Hospitality, Honesty, and the Neatness both of her
Person and House.

† The Place of her Residence being the greatest Sufferer, by the
loss of our Members of Parliament, which *London* now enjoys, many of
them having their Houses there, being the Suburb of *Edinburgh*
nearest the King's Palace ; this with the Death of Lucky *Wood* are
sufficient to make the Place ruinous.

Hear me ye Hills, and every Glen,
Ilk Craig, ilk Cleugh, and hollow Den,
And Echo shrill, that a' may ken
  The waefou Thud,
Be rackless Death, wha came unsenn ‡
  To Lucky *Wood*.

She's dead o'er true, she's dead and gane,
Left us and *Willie* § Burd alane,
To bleer and greet, to sob and mane,
  And rugg our Hair,
Because we'll ne'r see her again
  For evermair.

She gae'd as fait as a new Prin,
And kept her Housie snod and been ;
Her Peuther glanc'd upo' your Een
  Like Siller Plate ;
She was a donsie Wife and clean,
  Without Debate.

It did ane good to see her Stools,
Her Boord, Fire-side, and facing Tools ; ||
Rax, Chandlers, Tangs, and Fire-Shools,
  Basket wi' Bread.
Poor Facers ¶ now may chew Pea-hools,
  Since Lucky's dead.

‡ or *unsent for* ; There's nothing extraordinary in this, it being his common Custom, except in some few instances of late since the falling of the Bubbles.
§ Her Husband *William Wood*.
|| Stoups [or Pots] and Cups, so call'd from the *Facers. See* l. 29.
¶ The Facers were a Club of fair Drinkers who inclined rather to spend a Shilling on Ale than Twopence for Meat ; they had their Name from a Rule they observed of obliging themselves to throw all they left in the Cup in their own Faces : Wherefore to save their Face and Cloaths, they prudently suck'd the Liquor clean out.

She ne'er gae in a Lawin fause,**
Nor Stoups a Froath aboon the Hause,
Nor kept dow'd Tip within her Waw's,
        But reaming Swats ;
She never ran sour Jute, because
        It gee's the Batts.

She had the Gate sae well to please,
With *gratis* Beef, dry Fish, or Cheese ;
Which kept our Purses ay at Ease,
        And Health in Tift,
And lent her fresh Nine Gallon Trees
        A hearty Lift.

She ga'e us aft hail Legs o' Lamb,
And did nae hain her Mutton Ham ;
Than ay at *Yule*, when e'er we came,
        A bra' Goose Pye,
And was na that good Belly Baum ?
        Nane dare deny.

The Writer Lads fow well may mind her,
Furthy was she, her Luck design'd her
Their common Mither, sure nane kinder
        Ever brake Bread ;
She has na left her Make behind her,
        But now she's dead.

To the sma' Hours we aft sat still,
Nick'd round our Toasts and Snishing Mill ;
Good Cakes we wanted ne'r at Will,
        The best of Bread,
Which aften cost us mony a Gill
        To *Aikenhead*.††

** All this Verse is a fine Picture of an honest Ale-seller ; *A Rarity*.
 †† The Nether-bow Porter, to whom Lucky's Customers were often
obliged for opening the Port for them, when they staid out 'till the small
Hours after Midnight.

Cou'd our saut Tears like *Clyde* down rin,
And had we Cheeks like *Corra*'s Lin,‡‡
That a' the Warld might hear the Din
　　　Rair frae ilk Head ;
She was the Wale of a' her Kin,
　　　But now she's dead.

O Lucky *Wood*, 'tis hard to bear
The Loss ; but Oh ! we maun forbear :
Yet sall thy Memory be dear
　　　While blooms a Tree,
And after Ages Bairns will spear
　　　'Bout Thee and Me.

EPITAPH.

Beneath this Sod
Lies Lucky Wood,
Whom a' Men might put Faith in ;
Wha was na sweer,
While she winn'd here,
To cramm our Wames for naithing.

‡‡ A very high Precipice nigh *Lanerk*, over which the River of *Clyde* falls making a great Noise, which is heard some Miles off.

ELEGY

ON

JOHN COWPER Kirk-Treasurer's Man,*

ANNO 1714.

I wairn ye a' to greet and drone,
John Cowper's dead, Ohon ! Ohon !
To fill his Post, alake there's none,
    That with sic Speed
Could sa'r Sculdudry † out like *John*,
    But now he's dead.

He was right nacky in his Way,
And eydent baith be Night and Day,
He wi' the Lads his Part cou'd play,
    When right sair fleed,
He gart them good Bill-siller ‡ pay,
    But now he's dead.

* 'Tis necessary for the Illustration of this Elegy to Strangers to let them a little into the History of the Kirk-Treasurer and his Man ; The Treasurer is chosen every Year, a Citizen respected for Riches and Honesty ; he is vested with an absolute Power to seise and imprison the Girls that are too impatient to have on their green Gown before it be hem'd ; them he strictly examines, but no Liberty to be granted till a fair Account be given of these Persons they have obliged. It must be so : A List is frequently given sometimes of a Dozen or thereby of married or unmarried unfair Traders whom they secretly assisted in running their Goods, these his Lordship makes pay to some purpose according to their Ability, for the Use of the Poor : If the Lads be obstreperous, the Kirk-Sessions, and worst of all, the Stool of Repentance is threatned, a Punishment which few of any Spirit can bear.
    The Treasurer being changed every Year, never comes to be perfectly acquainted with the Affair ; but their general Servant continuing for a long Time, is more expert at discovering such Persons, and the Places of their Resort, which makes him capable to do himself and Customers both a good or an ill Turn. *John Cowper* maintain'd this Post with Activity and good Success for several Years.
    † In Allusion to a scent Dog, *Sa'r* from *Savour* or *Smell*, *Sculdudry* a Name commonly given to *whoring*.
    ‡ Bull-silver.
        She saw the Cow well serv'd, and took a Groat.—GAY.

Of Whore-hunting he gat his Fill,
And made be't mony Pint and Gill :
Of his braw Post he thought nae Ill,
  Nor did nae need,
Now they may mak a Kirk and Mill
  O't, since he's dead.

Altho he was nae Man of Weir,
Yet mony a ane, wi quaking Fear,
Durst scarce afore his Face appear,
  But hide their Head ;
The wylie Carle he gather'd Gear,
  And yet he's dead.

Ay now to some Part far awa,
Alas he's gane and left it a' !
May be to some sad Whilliwhaw §
  O' fremit Blood,
'Tis an ill Wind that dis na blaw
  Some Body good.

Fy upon Death, he was to blame
To whirle poor *John* to his lang Hame :
But tho his Arse be cauld, yet Fame,
  Wi' Tout of Trumpet,
Shall tell how *Cowper's* awfou Name
  Cou'd flie a Strumpet.

He kend the Bawds and Louns fou well,
And where they us'd to rant and reel,
He paukily on them cou'd steal,
  And spoil their Sport ;
Aft did they wish the muckle De'll
  Might tak him for't.

§ *Whilliwaw* is a kind of an insinuating deceitful Fellow, *Fremit Blood*, not a Kin, because he had then no legitimate Heirs of his own Body.

But ne'er a ane of them he spar'd,
E'en tho there was a drunken Laird
To draw his Sword, and make a Faird ‖
    In their Defence,
John quietly put them in the Guard
    To learn mair Sense.

There maun they ly till sober grown,
The Lad neist Day his Fault maun own ;
And to keep a' Things hush and low'n,
    He minds the Poor, ¶
Syne after a' his Ready's flown,[1]
    He damns the Whore.

And she, poor Jade, withoutten Din,
Is sent to *Leith*-Wynd Fit ** to spin,
With heavy Heart and Cleathing thin,
    And hungry Wame,
And ilky Month a well paid Skin,
    To mak her tame.

But now they may scoure up and down,
And safely gang their Wakes arown,
Spreading the Clap throw a' the Town,
    But Fear or Dread ;
For that great Kow to Bawd and Lown,
    John Cowper's dead.

Shame faw ye'r Chandler Chafts, †† O Death,
For stapping of *John Cowper*'s Breath ;
The Loss of him is publick Skaith :
    I dare well say,
To quat the Grip he was right laith
    This mony a Day.

‖ A Bustle like a Bully.   ¶ Pays hush Money to the Treasurer.
** The House of Correction at the Foot of *Leith*-Wynd, such as
Bridewell in *London*.

†† Lean or meager Cheeked, when the Bones appear like the Sides
or Corners of a Candlestick, which in Scots we call a *Chandler*.

[1] 1800 shown,

POSTSCRIPT.

Of umquhile *John* to lie or bann,
Shaws but ill Will, and looks right shan,
But some tell odd Tales of the Man,
      For Fifty Head
Can gi'e their Aith they've seen him gawn ‡‡
      Since he was dead.

Keek but up throw the *Stinking Stile,*||||
On *Sunday* Morning a wee While,
At the Kirk Door out frae an Isle,
      It will appear ;
But tak good Tent ye dinna file
      Ye'r Breeks for Fear.

For well we wat it is his Ghaist,
Wow, wad some Fouk that can do't best ¶¶
Speak till't, and hear what it confest ;
      'Tis a good Deed
To send a wand'ring Saul to rest
      Amang the Dead.

‡‡ The common People when they tell their Tales of Ghosts appearing, they say, he has been seen *gawn* or stalking.

|||| Opposite to this Place is the Door of the Church which he attends, being a Beadle.

¶¶ 'Tis another vulgar Notion, that a Ghost will not be laid to rest, till some Priest speak to it, and get Account what disturbs it.

ELEGY

ON

*MAGGY JOHNSTON,**

who died *Anno* 1711.

AULD Reeky † mourn in Sable Hue,
Let Fouth of Tears dreep like *May* Dew,
To braw Tippony ‡ bid Adieu,
    Which we with Greed
Bended as fast as she cou'd brew,
    But ah ! she's dead.

To tell the Truth now *Maggy* dang,§
Of Customers she had a Bang ;
For Lairds and Souters a' did gang
    To drink bedeen,
The Barn and Yard was aft sae thrang,
    We took the Green.

And there by Dizens we lay down,
Syne sweetly ca'd the Healths arown,
To bonny Lasses black or brown,
    As we loo'd best ;
In Bumpers we dull Cares did drown,
    And took our Rest.

---

  * *Maggy Johnston* liv'd about a Mile Southward of *Edinburgh*, kept a little Farm, and had a particular Art of brewing a small Sort of Ale agreeable to the Taste, very white, clear and intoxicating, which made People who lov'd to have a good Pennyworth for their Money be her frequent Customers. And many others of every Station, sometimes for Diversion, thought it no Affront to be seen in her Barn or Yard.

  † A Name the Country People give *Edinburgh* from the Cloud of Smoak or Reek that is always impending over it.

  ‡ She sold the *Scots* Pint, which is near two Quarts *English*, for Twopence.

  § He *dings*, or *dang*, is a Phrase which means *to excel or get the better*.

When in our Poutch we fand some Clinks,
And took a Turn o'er *Bruntsfield-Links*, ||
Aften in *Maggy's* at Hy-jinks, ¶
    We guzl'd Scuds,
Till we cou'd scarce wi' hale-out Drinks
    Cast aff our Duds.

We drank and drew, and fill'd again,
O wow but we were blyth and fain !
When ony had their Count mistain,
    O it was nice,
To hear us a' cry, Pike ye'r Bain, **
    And spell ye'r Dice.

Fou closs we us'd to drink and rant,
Until we did baith glowre and gaunt,
And pish and spew, and yesk and maunt,
    Right swash I true ;
Then of auld Stories we did cant
    When we were fou.

|| Fields between *Edinburgh* and *Maggy's*, where the Citizens commonly play at the Gowff.

¶ A drunken Game, or new Project to drink and be rich ; thus, The Quaff or Cup is fill'd to the Brim, then one of the Company takes a Pair of Dice, and after crying *Hy-jinks*, he throws them out : The Number he casts up points out the Person must drink, he who threw, beginning at himself Number One, and so round till the Number of the Person agree with that of the Dice (which may fall upon himself if the Number be within Twelve ;) then he sets the Dice to him, or bids him take them : He on whom they fall is obliged to drink, or pay a small Forfeiture in Money ; then throws, and so on : But if he forget to cry *Hy-jinks* he pays a Forfeiture into the Bank. Now he on whom it falls to drink, if there be any Thing in Bank worth drawing, gets it all if he drinks. Then with a great Deal of Caution he empties his Cup, sweeps up the Money, and orders the Cup to be fill'd again, and then throws ; for if he err in the Articles, he loses the Privilege of drawing the Money. The Articles are, (1) Drink, (2) Draw, (3) Fill, (4) Cry *Hy-jinks*, (5) Count just, (6) Chuse your doublet Man, *viz.* when two equal Numbers of the Dice is thrown, the Person whom you chuse must pay a Double of the common Forfeiture, and so must you when the Dice is in his Hand. A rare Project this, and no Bubble I can assure you ; for a covetous Fellow may save Money, and get himself as drunk as he can desire in less than an Hour's Time.

** Is a Cant Phrase, when one leaves a little in the Cup, he is advised to pike his bone, *i.e.* Drink it clean out.

Whan we were weary'd at the Gowff,
Then *Maggy Johnston's* was our Howff ;
Now a' our Gamesters may sit dowff,
  Wi' Hearts like Lead,
Death wi' his Rung rax'd her a Yowff,††
  And sae she died.

Maun we be forc'd thy Skill to tine ?
For which we will right sair repine ;
Or hast thou left to Bairns of thine
  The pauky Knack
Of brewing Ale amaist like Wine,
  That gar'd us crack.

Sae brawly did a Pease-scon Toast
Biz i' the Queff, and flie the Frost ; ‡‡
There we gat fou wi' little Cost,
  And muckle Speed,
Now wae worth Death, our Sport's a' lost,
  Since *Maggy's* dead.

Ae Simmer Night §§ I was sae fou,
Amang the Riggs I geed to spew ;
Syne down on a green Bawk, I trow
  I took a Nap,
And soucht a Night Balillilow,
  As sound's a Tap.

And when the Dawn begoud to glow,
I hirsl'd up my dizzy Pow,

†† Reach'd her a Blow.
‡‡ Or fright the Frost or Coldness out of it.
§§ The two following Stanzas are a true Narrative.

  On that slid Place where I 'maist brake my Bains,
  To be a Warning I set up twa Stains,
  That nane may venture there as I have done,
  Unless wi' frosted Nails he clink his Shoon.

Frae 'mang the Corn like Wirricow,
      Wi' Bains sae sair,
And ken'd nae mair than if a Ew
      How I came there.

Some said it was the Pith of Broom
That she stow'd in her Masking-loom,
Which in our Heads rais'd sic a Foom,
      Or some wild Seed,
Which aft the Chaping Stoup did toom,
      But fill'd our Head.

But now since 'tis sae that we must
Not in the best Ale put our Trust,
But whan we're auld return to Dust
      Without Remead,
Why shou'd we tak it in Disgust
      That *Maggy*'s dead.

Of warldly Comforts she was rife,
And liv'd a lang and hearty Life,
Right free of Care, or Toil, or Strife,
      Till she was stale,
And ken'd to be a kanny Wife
      At brewing Ale.

Then farewell *Maggy* douce and fell,
Of Brewers a' thou boor the Bell ;
Let a' thy Gossies yelp and yell,
      And without Feed,
Guess whether ye're in Heaven or Hell,
      They're sure ye're dead.

EPITAPH.

O Rare MAGGY JOHNSTON.

LUCKY SPENCE'S * LAST ADVICE.

THREE Times the Carline grain'd and rifted,
Then frae the Cod her Pow she lifted,
In bawdy Policy well gifted,
  When she now faun,
That Death na langer wad be shifted,
  She thus began :

My loving Lasses, I maun leave ye,
But dinna wi' ye'r Greeting grieve me,
Nor wi' your Draunts and Droning deave me,
  But bring's a Gill ;
For Faith, my Bairns, ye may believe me,
  'Tis 'gainst my Will.

O black Ey'd *Bess* and mim Mou'd *Meg,*†
O'er good to work or yet to beg ;
Lay Sunkots up for a sair Leg,
  For whan ye fail,
Ye'r Face will not be worth a Feg,
  Nor yet ye'r Tail.

Whan e'er ye meet a Fool that's fow,
That ye're a Maiden gar him trow,
Seem nice, but stick to him like Glew ;
  And whan set down,
Drive at the Jango till he spew,
  Syn he'll sleep soun.

---

* Lucky *Spence*, a famous Bawd who flourished for several Years about the Beginning of the Eighteenth Century ; she had her Lodgings near *Holyrood-house* ; she made many a benefit Night to herself, by putting a Trade in the Hands of young Lasses that had a little Pertness, strong Passions, Abundance of Laziness, and no Fore-thought.

† Expresses an affected Modesty, by a preciseness about the Mouth.

Whan he's asleep, then dive and catch
His ready Cash, his Rings or Watch ;
And gin he likes to light his Match ‡
    At your Spunk-box,
Ne'er stand to let the fumbling Wretch
    E'en take the Pox.

Cleek a' ye can be Hook or Crook,
Ryp ilky Poutch frae Nook to Nook ;
Be sure to truff his Pocket-book,
    Saxty Pounds *Scots*
Is nae deaf Nits : § In little Bouk
    Lie great Bank-Notes.

To get a Mends of whinging Fools,‖
That's frighted for Repenting-Stools,
Wha often, whan their Metal cools,
    Turn sweer to pay,
Gar the Kirk-Boxie hale the Dools ¶
    Anither Day.

But dawt Red Coats, and let them scoup,
Free for the Fou of cutty Stoup ; **
To gee them up, ye need na hope
    E'er to do well :
They'll rive ye'r Brats and kick your Doup,
    And play the Deel.

    ‡ I could give a large Annotation on this Sentence, but do not incline to explain every thing, lest I disoblige future Criticks, by leaving nothing for them to do.
    § or *empty Nuts* ; This is a negative manner of saying a thing is substantial.
    ‖ To be revenged ; *of whindging Fools*, Fellows who wear the wrong side of their Faces outmost, Pretenders to Sanctity, who love to be smugling in a Corner.
    ¶ Delate them to the Kirk-Treasurer. *Hale the Dools* is a Phrase used at Foot-ball, where the Party that gains the *Goal* or *Dool* is said to hail it or win the Game, and so draws the Stake.
    ** Little Pot, *i.e.* a Gill of Brandy.

There's ae sair Cross attends the Craft,
That curst Correction-house, where aft
Vild Hangy's Taz †† ye'r Riggings saft
    Makes black and blae,
Enough to pit a Body daft ;
    But what'll ye say.‡‡

Nane gathers Gear withoutten Care,
Ilk Pleasure has of Pain a Skare ;
Suppose then they should tirle ye bare,
    And gar ye sike,[1]
E'en learn to thole ; 'tis very fair
    Ye're Nibour like.

Forby, my Looves, count upo' Losses,
Ye'r Milk-white Teeth and Cheeks like Roses,
Whan Jet-black Hair and Brigs of Noses,
    Faw down wi' Dads
To keep your Hearts up 'neath sic Crosses,
    Set up for Bawds.

Wi' well crish'd Loofs I hae been canty,
Whan e'er the Lads wad fain ha'e faun t'ye ;
To try the auld Game *Taunty Raunty*,
    Like Coofers keen,
They took Advice of me your Aunty,
    If ye were clean.

Then up I took my Siller Ca'
And whistl'd benn §§ whiles ane, whiles twa ;

†† If they perform not the Task assign'd them, they are whipt by the Hangman.
‡‡ The Emphasis of this Phrase, like many others, cannot be understood but by a Native.
§§ *But* and *Ben* signify different Ends or Rooms of a House ; to gang *But* and *Ben* is to go from one end of the House to the other.

---

[1] 1728 fike,

Roun'd in his Lug,|||| That there was a
    Poor Country *Kate*,
As halesom as the Well of *Spaw*,
    But unka blate.

Sae whan e'er Company came in,
And were upo' a merry Pin,
I slade away wi' little Din,
    And muckle Mense,
Left Conscience Judge,¶¶ it was a' ane
    To Lucky *Spence*.

My Bennison come on good Doers,
Who spend their Cash on Bawds and Whores ;
May they ne'er want the Wale of Cures
    For a fair Snout :
Foul fa' the Quacks wha that Fire smoors,*
    And puts nae out.

My Malison light ilka Day
On them that drink, and dinna pay,
But tak a Snack and rin away ;
    May't be their Hap
Never to want a *Gonorrhœa*,
    Or rotten Clap.

Lass gi'e us in anither Gill,
A Mutchken, Jo, let's tak our Fill ;
Let Death syne registrate his Bill
    Whan I want Sense,
I'll slip away with better Will,
    Quo' Lucky *Spence*.

|||| Whisper'd in his Ear.

¶¶ It was her usual Way of vindicating herself to tell ye, *When Company came to her House, could she be so uncivil as to turn them out ? If they did any bad thing*, said she, *between GOD and their Conscience be't*.

* Such Quacks as bind up the external Symptoms of the Pox, and drive it inward to the strong Holds, whence it is not so easily expelled.

MY PEGGY IS A YOUNG THING.

[To the Tune of *The Wauking of the Faulds*.]

[From the Ed. of 1800.]

My Peggy is a young thing,
   Just enter'd in her teens,
Fair as the day, and sweet as May,
Fair as the day, and always gay :
My Peggy is a young thing,
   And I'm not very auld,
Yet well I like to meet her at
   The wauking of the fauld.

My Peggy speaks sae sweetly,
   Whene'er we meet alane,
I wish nae wair to lay my care,
I wish nae mair of a' that's rare,
My Peggy speaks sae sweetly,
   To all the lave I'm cauld ;
But she gars a' my spirits glow,
   At wauking of the fauld.

My Peggy smiles sae kindly,
   Whene'er I whisper love,
That I look down on a' the town,
That I look down upon a crown.
My Peggy smiles sae kindly,
   It makes me blyth and bauld ;
And nathing gi'es me sic delight
   As wauking of the fauld.

My Peggy sings sae saftly,
   When on my pipe I play,
By a' the rest it is confest,
By a' the rest that she sings best.

My Peggy sings sae saftly,
    And in her sangs are tald,
With innocence the wale of sense,
    At wauking of the fauld.
[From *The Gentle Shepherd*.]

THIS IS NO MY AIN HOUSE.

[From the Ed. of 1800.]

THIS is no mine ain house,
    I ken by the rigging o't ;
Since with my love I've changèd vows,
    I dinna like the bigging o't :
For now that I'm young Robie's bride,
And mistress of his fire-side,
Mine ain house I'll like to guide,
    And please me with the trigging o't.

Then farewell to my father's house,
    I gang where love invites me ;
The strictest duty this allows,
    When love with honour meets me.
When Hymen moulds us into ane,
My Robie's nearer than my kin,
And to refuse him were a sin,
    Sae lang's he kindly treats me.

When I'm in mine ain house,
    True love shall be at hand ay,
To make me still a prudent spouse,
    And let my man command ay ;
Avoiding ilka cause of strife,
The common pest of married life,
That makes ane wearied of his wife,
    And breaks the kindly band ay.

THE CARLE HE CAME O'ER THE CROFT.

[From the Ed. of 1800.]

THE carle he came o'er the croft,
    And his beard new shaven,
He look'd at me as he'd been daft,
    The carle trows that I wad hae him.
Howt awa ! I winna hae him,
    Na forsooth I winna hae him,
For a' his beard's new shaven,
    Ne'er a bit will I hae him.

A siller broach he gae me niest,
    To fasten on my curtchea nooked ;
I wor'd a wee upon my breast,
    But soon, alake ! the tongue o't crooked ;
And sae may his : I winna hae him ;
    Na forsooth I winna hae him ;
Ane twice a bairn's a lass's jest ;
    Sae ony fool for me may hae him.

THE carle has nae fault but ane,
    For he has land and dollars plenty ;
But waes me for him ! skin and bane
    Is no for a plump lass of twenty.
Howt awa ! I winna hae him,
    Na forsooth I winna hae him ;
What signifies his dirty riggs
    And cash without a man with them ?

BUT shou'd my canker'd daddy gar
    Me take him 'gainst my inclination,
I warn the fumbler to beware,
    That antlers dinna claim their station.

Howt awa ! I winna hae him,
    Na forsooth I winna hae him ;
I'm flee'd to crack the haly band,
    Sae Lawty says I shou'd na hae him.

O MITHER DEAR ! I 'GIN TO FEAR.

[From the Ed. of 1800.]

CHORUS.

Up stairs, down stairs,
    Timber stairs fear me ;
I'm laith to ly a' night my lane,
    And Johny's bed sae near me.

O mither dear ! I 'gin to fear,
    Tho' I'm baith good and bonny,
I winna keep ; for in my sleep
    I start and dream of Johny.
When Johny then comes down the glen
    To woo me, dinna hinder ;
But with content gi'e your consent,
    For we twa ne'er can sinder.

Better to marry than miscarry,
    For shame and skaith's the clink o't ;
To thole the dool, to mount the stool,
    I downa bide to think o't :
Sae while 'tis time, I'll shun the crime,
    That gars poor Epps gae whinging,
With hainches fow, and een sae blew,
    To a' the bedrals bindging.

Had Eppy's apron bidden down,
    The kirk wad ne'er a kend it ;
But when the word's gane thro' the town,
    Alake ! how can she mend it ?

D

Now Tam man face the minister,
    And she man mount the pillar ;
And that's the way that they man gae,
    For poor folk has nae siller.

Now ha'd ye'r tongue, my daughter young,
    Replied the kindly mither ;
Get Johny's hand in haly band,
    Syne wap ye'r wealth together.
I'm o' the mind, if he be kind,
    Ye'll do your part discreetly,
And prove a wife will gar his life
    And barrel run right sweetly.

UP IN THE AIR.

Now the Sun's gane out o' Sight,
Beet the Ingle, and snuff the Light :
In Glens the Fairies skip and dance,
And Witches wallop o'er to *France*,
                Up in the Air
                On my bonny grey Mare.
And I see her yet, and I see her yet,
                Up in, *&c.*

THE Wind's drifting Hail and Sna'
O'er frozen Hags like a Foot Ba',
Nae Starns keek throw the Azure Slit,
'Tis cauld and mirk as ony Pit,
                The Man i' the Moon
                Is carowsing aboon,
D'ye see, d'ye see, d'ye see him yet.
                The Man, *&c.*

TAKE your Glass to clear your Een,
'Tis the *Elixir* hales the Spleen,
Baith Wit and Mirth it will inspire,
And gently puffs the Lover's Fire,
              Up in the Air,
              It drives away Care,
Ha'e wi'ye, ha'e wi'ye, and ha'e wi'ye Lads yet,
              Up in, &c.

STEEK the Doors, keep out the Frost,
Come *Willy* gi'es about ye'r Tost,
Til't Lads, and lilt it out,
And let us ha'e a blythsom Bowt,
              Up wi't there, there,
              Dinna cheat, but drink fair,
Huzza, Huzza, and Huzza Lads yet,
              Up wi't, &c.

THE WIDOW.

THE Widow can bake, and the Widow can brew,
The Widow can shape, and the Widow can shew,
And mony braw Things the Widow can do ;
     Then have at the Widow, my Laddie.
With Courage attack her baith early and late,
To kiss her and clap her ye mauna be blate :
Speak well, and do better ; for that's the best Gate
     To win a young Widow, my Laddie.

THE Widow she's youthfu', and never ae Hair
The war of the wearing, and has a good Skair
Of everything lovely ; she's witty and fair,
     And has a rich Jointure, my Laddie.

What cou'd ye wish better your Pleasure to crown,
Than a Widow, the bonniest Toast in the Town,
With nathing, but draw in your Stool, and sit down,
    And sport with the Widow, my Laddie.

THEN till her, and kill her with Courtesy dead,
Tho' stark Love and Kindness be all ye can plead ;
Be heartsome and airy, and hope to succeed
    With a bonny gay Widow, my Laddie.
Strike Iron while 'tis het, if ye'd have it to wald,
For Fortune ay favours the Active and Bauld,
But ruines the Woer that's thowless and cauld,
    Unfit for the Widow, my Laddie.

NANNY O.

WHILE some for Pleasure pawn their Health,
    'Twixt *Lais* and the *Bagnio*,
I'll save my self, and without Stealth
    Kiss and caress my *Nanny-O*.
She bids more fair t'ingage a *Jove*,
    Then *Leda* did or *Danae-O ;* *
Were I to paint the Queen of Love,
    None else shou'd sit but *Nanny-O*.

How joyfully my Spirits rise,
    When dancing she moves finely—O,
I guess what Heav'n is by her Eyes,
    Which sparkle so divinely O.
Attend my Vow, ye Gods, while I
    Breath in the blest *Britannio*,

* Two Beauties to whom *Jove* made Love ; to one in the Figure
of a Swan, to the other in a Golden Shower.

None's Happiness I shall envy,
As long's ye grant me *Nanny-O*.

CHORUS.

My bonny, bonny Nanny-O,
My loving charming Nanny-O,
I care not tho the World do know
How dearly I love Nanny-O.

THE LASS OF PEATTIE'S MILL.

The Lass of *Peattie*'s Mill,
So bonny, blyth and gay,
In spite of all my Skill,
She stole my Heart away.
When tedding of the Hay
Bare-headed on the Green,
Love 'midst her Locks did play,
And wanton'd in her Een.

Her Arms white, round and smooth,
Breasts rising in their Dawn,
To Age it wou'd give Youth,
To press 'em with his Hand.
Thro' all my Spirits ran
An Extasy of Bliss,
When I such Sweetness fand
Wrapt in a balmy Kiss.

Without the Help of Art,
Like Flowers which grace the Wild,
She did her Sweets impart,
When e'er she spoke or smil'd.
Her Looks they were so mild,
Free from affected Pride,
She me to Love beguil'd ;
I wish'd her for my Bride.

O had I all that Wealth
Hopeton's high Mountains * fill
Insur'd long Life and Health,
And Pleasure at my Will ;
I'd promise and fulfill,
That none but bonny She,
The Lass of *Peattie*'s Mill
Shou'd share the same wi' me.

* Thirty three Miles South-west of *Edinburgh*, where the Right
Honourable the Earl of *Hopeton*'s Mines of Gold and Lead are.

BESSY BELL AND MARY GRAY.

O *Bessy Bell* and *Mary Gray*
They are twa bonny Lasses,
They bigg'd a Bower on yon Burn-brae,
And theek'd it o'er wi' Rashes.
Fair *Bessy Bell* I loo'd yestreen,
And thought I ne'er cou'd alter ;
But *Mary Gray*'s twa pawky Een,
They gar my Fancy falter.

Now *Bessy*'s Hair's like a Lint Tap,
She smiles like a *May* Morning,
When *Phœbus* starts frae *Thetis*' Lap,
The Hills with Rays adorning :
White is her Neck, saft is her Hand,
Her Waste and Feet's fow genty,
With ilka Grace she can command,
Her Lips, O wow ! they're dainty.

AND *Mary*'s Locks are like the Craw,
Her Eye like Diamonds glances ;
She's aye sae clean, red-up and braw,
She kills when e'er she dances :

Blyth as a Kid, with Wit at Will,
She blooming, tight [1] and tall is ;
And guides her Airs sae gracefou still,
O *Jove!* she's like thy *Pallas*.

DEAR *Bessy Bell* and *Mary Gray*,
Ye unco sair oppress us,
Our Fancies jee between you twae,
Ye are sic bonny Lasses :
Wae's me, for baith I canna get,
To ane by Law we're stented ;
Then I'll draw Cuts and take my Fate,
And be with ane contented.

[1] [I have ventured to remove at least *one* of the ambiguities of this unfortunate stanza by supplying the comma after " blooming."—ED.]

FOR THE SAKE OF SOMEBODY.

[From the Ed. of 1800.]

For the sake of somebody,
    For the sake of somebody,
I cou'd wake a winter night
    For the sake of somebody.
I am gawn to seek a wife,
    I am gawn to buy a plaidy ;
I have three stane of woo,
    Carling, is thy daughter ready ?
For the sake of somebody, &c.

Betty, lassie, say't thysell,
    Tho' thy dame be ill to shoo,
First we'll buckle, then we'll tell,
    Let her flyte and syne come too :
What signifies a mither's gloom,
    When love and kisses come in play ?
Shou'd we wither in our bloom,
    And in simmer mak nae hay ?
For the sake, &c.

SHE.

Bonny lad, I carena by,
 Tho' I try my luck with thee,
Since ye are content to tye
 The haff mark bridal band wi' me :
I'll slip hame and wash my feet,
 And steal on linnings fair and clean,
Syne at the trysting-place we'll meet,
 To do but what my dame has done.
For the sake, &c.

HE.

Now my lovely Betty gives
 Consent in sic a heartsome gate,
It me frae a' my care relieves,
 And doubts that gart me aft look blate :
Then let us gang and get the grace,
 For they that have an appetite
Shou'd eat ; and lovers shou'd embrace ;
 If these be faults, 'tis nature's wyte.
For the sake, &c.

ANN THOU WERE MY AIN THING.

Ann thou were my ain Thing,
I would love thee, I would love thee ;
Ann thou were my ain Thing,
How dearly would I love thee.

LIKE Bees that suck the Morning Dew
Frae Flowers of sweetest Scent and Hew,
Sae wad I dwell upo' thy Mou,
 And gar the Gods envý [1] me.
  Ann thou were, &c.

[1] Accent supplied.—[Ed.]   Cp. *Nanny O*, l. 15, p. 61.

SAE lang's I had the Use of Light,
[I'd on] thy Beauties feast my Sight,
Syne in saft Whispers through the Night,
   I'd tell how much I loo'd thee.

      Ann thou were, &c.

How fair and ruddy is my *Jean* !
She moves a Goddess o'er the Green :
Were I a King, thou shou'd be Queen,
   Nane but my sell aboon thee.

      Ann thou were, &c.

I'D grasp thee to this Breast of mine,
Whilst thou, like Ivy, or the Vine,
Around my stronger Limbs shou'd twine,
   Form'd hardy to defend thee.

      Ann thou were, &c.

TIME's on the Wing, and will not stay,
In shining Youth let's make our Hay,
Since Love admits of no Delay,
   O ! let na Scorn undo thee.

      Ann thou were, &c.

WHILE Love does at his Altar stand,
Hae there my Heart, gi'e me thy Hand,
And with ilk Smile thou shalt command
   The Will of him wha loves thee.

      Ann thou were, &c.

GLOSSARY

The majority of the definitions in this short glossary are taken from the glossary of Ruddiman's edition of 1721-28. Where that is deficient, I have drawn upon Chalmers' edition of 1800, and, in rare cases, supplied the defect myself.

A

Aboon, Above.
Asks, [Newts].
Auldfarran, Ingenious.
Auldgabbet. See *Gabby*.

B

Back-sey, A Surloin.
Bairn, Child.
Balillilow, [Lullaby. A night's sleep].
Bang, v. " an Action of Haste " ; *sb.* " a great Number."
Bann, Curse.
Batts, Colick.
Bauch, Sorry, indifferent.
Bauld, Bold.
Bawk, A rafter, joist : likewise, the space between corn fields. [1800.]
Bedrals, [Church-officers].
Beek, Bask.
Been, *bein*, Wealthy. *A been House*, A warm, well furnished one.
Begoud, Began.
Bend, *ben*, Drink hard.
Bent, The open Field.
Bield, A Shelter.
Big, *bigg'd*, *bigging*, Build, built, building.
Billies, Brothers, [cronies].
Bill-siller. See Notes, p. 42.

Bindging, [Cringing].
Binks, [Benches].
Birn, A burnt Mark.
Birns, The Stalks of burnt Heath.
Birr, Force.
Bittle, A wooden Mell for beating Hemp, or a Fuller's Club.
Biz, Hiss.
Blae, Pale blew, the Colour of the Skin when bruised.
Blate, Bashful.
Blatt'ring, *blatran*, [Making] a rattling Noise.
Blawart, A blue flower that grows among corn. [1800.]
Bleez, Blaze.
Bodles, One sixth of a Penny *English*.
Boss, Empty.
Bourd, Jest or Dalley.
Bowk, Bulk.
Borrows-toun, [A town with borough rights].
Brae, The Side of a Hill, Bank of a River.
Brats, Rags.
Brock, A Badger.
Busked, [Adorned, dressed to attract].
Butt and ben. See Notes, p. 52.

C

Campsho, Stern, grim, of a distorted Countenance.

Canny, kanny, [Careful, shrewd].

Cant, To tell merry old Tales.

Canty, [*cantily*], Chearful and merry, [cheerfully].

Carle, carlie, An old Word for a Man.

Carline, An old Woman.

Chandler, [Candlestick. *Chandler Chafts,* see Notes, p. 44].

Chaping-stoup, An Ale Measure or Stoup, somewhat less than an *English* Quart.

Chiel, chield, A general term, like Fellow, used sometimes with Respect ; as, *He's a very good Chiel* ; and contemptuously, *That Chiel.*

Chorking, The noise made by the feet when the shoes are full of water. [1800.]

Clash, Chat.

Claver, To speak Nonsense.

Cleugh, A Den betwixt Rocks.

Clinks, Coins, money. [1800.]

Clout, [Mend].

Cod, A Pillow.

Coof, A stupid Fellow.

Corky, [An empty-headed fellow].

Cow'd, [Culled, pulled].

Cowp, A Company of People ; as, merry, senseless, corky *Cowp.*

Craig, A rock ; the neck. [1800.]

Crap, [Crest].

Crish'd, crishy, [Greased, greasy].

Croil, A crooked Dwarf.

Cunzie, Coin.

Cutty, Short.

D

Dad, To beat one Thing against another. *He fell with a Dad.*

Daffin, -ine, Folly. Wagrie.

Daft, Foolish ; and sometimes wanton.

Dang, Did ding, Beat. Thrust. Drive.

Darrin, [Daring].

Dawt, To cocker, and caress with tenderness. [*Dawted,* petted.]

Dead, [Death].

Deave, To stun the Ears with Noise.

Decreet, [Archaic term in Sc. law : decision, determination].

Dees, Dairy [1728 *Diary*] Maids.

Dikes, [Ditches ; but more commonly in Scots, stone boundary walls].

Ding. See *Dang.*

Doited, Dozed or crazy, as in old Age.

Donsie, Affectedly neat. Clean, when applied to any little Person.

Dool, Pain. Grief.

Doup, The Arse, the small Remains of a Candle, the Bottom of an Egg-shell. *Better haff Egg as toom dowp.*

Douse, dousser, Solid. Grave. Prudent.

Dow, To will, to incline, to thrive.

Dowff, Mournful, wanting Vivacity.

Dowy, Melancholy. Sad. Doleful.

Drant, To speak slow, after a sighing Manner.

Dreep, [Drip].

Dribs, Drops.

Drole, [Droll, strange, odd].

Duds, Rags. [1800.]

Dung, Defeat. [1800 : driven, down, overcome.]

E

Eard, Earth. The Ground.

Elritch, Wild. Hideous. Uninhabited, except by imaginary Ghosts.

Ether, An Adder.

Even'd, Compared. [1800.]

Eydent, Diligent. Laborious.

F

Fa', [*v.* 1, Fall, 2, Come in for] ; *sb.* A Trap, such as is used for catching Rats or Mice.

Facers, facing - tools, See Notes, p. 39.

Fain, This Word used in England expresses a Desire or Willingness to do a Thing; as, *Fain would I.* Besides its being used in the same Sense with us, it likewise means Joyful, tickled with Pleasure. As, *As fain as a Fidler.*

Faird. See Notes, p. 44.

Fait, Neat. In good Order.

Fash, fashous, Vex or Trouble. Troublesome.

Fauld, [Sheepfold].

Faun, [Fallen].

Fause, False. [1800.]

Feck, A Part, Quantity; as, Maist Feck, The greatest Number. *Nae Feck,* Very few.

Feckfu', Able. Active.

Feckless, Feeble, little and weak.

Feed, Fend. Hatred. Quarrel.

Feer, [Fair (?)].

Fen, Fend, Shift. *Fending,* Living by Industry. *Make a Fen,* Fall upon Methods.

Ferly, Wonder.

File, To defile or dirty.

Fistle, To stir. A Stir.

Flee, fley, flie, flied, To affright. *Fleyt,* Afraid or terrified.

Flyte, To scold. Chide.

Foom, [Fume].

Forby, Besides.

Forfairn, Abused. Bespatter'd.

Fouth, Abundance. Plenty.

Fow, [Full].

Fremit, Strange. Not a Kin.

Furthy, Forward.

G

Gab, The Mouth, To prat. *Gab sae gash.*

Gabby, One of a ready and easy Expression. The same with *auld Gabbet.*

Gaffaw, A hearty loud Laughter.

Gar, To cause, make, or force.

Gash, Solid, Sagacious. One with a long out Chin, we call *Gash Gabbet,* or *Gash Beard.*

Gate, Way.

Gaunt, Yawn.

Gaw, To take the pet, to be galled. [Hence, *Gaw'd.*]

Genty, Handsome, Genteel.

Gilly, [dim. of *Gill*].

Gin, If.

Girn, To Grin, Snarl.

Gleg, Sharp, Quick, Active.

Glunsh, To hang the Brow and grumble.

Goss, gossy, gossie, Gossip.

Gove, To look broad and stedfast, holding up the Face.

Gowans, Dazies.

Gowl, A Howling, to bellow and cry.

Greet, To weep. *Grat,* Wept.

H

Haff mark bridal band, Clandestine marriage.

Hags, Hacks, peat-pits, or breaks in mossy ground; portions of copsewood regularly cut. [1800.]

Hain, To save, manage narrowly. [*Haining,* saving.]

Hainches, [Haunches].

Haith, [An expostulation].

Hally, [Holy].

Hangy, [The public Hangman. See Notes, p. 52].

Hanty, Convenient, handsome.

Hause, Haws, The Throat, or fore Part of the Neck.

Heez, To lift up a heavy Thing a little.

Heezy, A good lift.

Highs and hows, [Heights and hollows].

Hirsle, To move as with a rustling Noise.

Hog-wedders, [*Hog,* a sheep of two years old. *Wedder,* wether].

Houghs, Hows. See *Highs and hows.*

Howff, A haunt, or accustomed rendezvous. [1800.]

Howms, holms, Plains on riversides. [1800.]

Hy-jinks. See Notes, p. 47.

I

Ilka, ilky, Each, every.

Ill - willy, [Unfriendly, ill - intended].

Ingine, Genius. [1800.]

J

Jango, [Drink (?)].

Jee, To incline to one Side. *a Jee,* [with a bias].

Jo, Sweet-heart.

Jute, Sour or dead Liquor.

K

Kebuck, A Cheese.

Kedgy, Jovial.

Kelt, Cloth with a freeze, commonly made of native black wool. [1800.]

Kiltit, Tuck'd up.

Kirk-boxie. See Notes, p. 51.

Kirn, A Churn. *Idem,** To churn. [* 1728 *Item,*]

Kitchen, All Sort of Eatables except Bread.

Kittle, To tickle, ticklish.

Knoost, A large lump. [1800.]

L

Laigh, laigher, low, [lower].

Laith, Loth. [1800.]

Landart, The Country, or belonging to it. Rustick.

Lang-kail, Coleworts uncut down.

Lav'rock, The Lark.

Lawin, A Tavern Reckoning.

Lawty, Justice, Fidelity, Honesty.

Lear, Learning, to learn.

Leugh, Laughed.

Lift, The Sky or Firmament.

Linking, linkan, Walking speedily.

Loof, The Hollow of the Hand.

Loun, lown, Rogue, Whore, Villain.

Lug, Ear, Handle of a Pot or Vessel.

M

Maik, make, Match, Equal.

Masking-loom, Mash-Vat.

Maunt, To stammer in Speech.

Mense, Discretion, Sobriety, good Breeding. *Mensefou,* Mannerly.

Menzie, Company of Men, Army, Assembly, one's Followers.

Messen, A little Dog, Lap-dog.

Mint, Aim, endeavour.

Mirk, Dark.

Mutchken, An *English* Pint.

N

Nacky, Clever, action in small Affairs.

Nay-says, [Denials, refusals].

Neist, Next.

Nick, To bite or cheat. *Nicked,* Cheated ; also as a cant Word, to drink heartily ; as, *He nicks fine.*

Nignyes, Trifles. [1800.]

Nits, Nuts. See Notes, p. 51.

Nodles, [Heads].

O

Ora, orra, Any thing over what is needful. [1800.]

P

Paughty, Proud, haughty.

Pauky, pawky, Witty or sly in Word or Action, without any Harm or bad Designs.

Pegh, To pant. [*Peghing,* panting.]

Pelts, [Blows].

Pettle, To dandle, feed, cherish, flatter. [1800.]

Pin, [Riot, horse-play, drunken revel.]

Pingle, To contend, strive or work hard.

Pirny, from *Pirn,* The Spool or Quill within the Shutle, which receives the Yarn. *Pirny,* (Cloath or a Web) of unequal Threads or Colours, stripped.

Pleugh, [Plough].

Poortith, Poverty.

Pow, The poll, the head. [1800.]

Prin, A Pin.

Pullieses, Pulleys. [1800.]

Q

Quat, to quit. [1800.]

Quate, [Quiet].

Queff, A flat wooden drinking-cup formed of staves. [1800.]

R

Rash-busses, [Clumps of rushes].

Rashes, Rushes.

Reese, roose, To commend, extoll.

Ribs, [The bars of the fire-place].

Rift, To belch.

Rigging, The Back, or Rig-back, The Top or Ridge of a House.

Riggs, Of corn, ridges. [1800.]

Ripe, To search. [To poke into.]

Rottle, [Stagger].

Roun'd, [Whispered].

Routh, rowth, Plenty.

Rug, To pull, take away by Force.

Rugget, [Rugged].

Runkled, from *Runkle,* a Wrinkle. *Runckle,* To rufle.

S

Sa'r, Savour or Smell.

Scar, The bare Places on the Sides of Hills washen down with Rains.

Scowp, To leap or move hastily from one Place to another.

Scuds, Ale. A late Name given it by the Benders, perhaps from its easy and clever Motion.

Sculdudry, [Whoredom. Immoral talk or behaviour. See Notes, p. 42.

Shan, Pitiful, silly, poor.

Sheers, [Scissors].

Shew, [To sew].

Shochling, [Shambling].

Shottle, A Drawer.

Shyrest, from *Shire,* Clear, thin. We call thin Cloath, or clear liquor, *Shire.* Also a clever Wag, *A Shire lick.*

Sike, A Rill or Rivulet, commonly dry in Summer. [*v.* To sigh.]

Sinder, [To sunder, part].

Sinsyne, Since that Tyme. *Lang sinsyne,* Long ago.

Skair, Share.

Skaith, Hurt, Damage, Loss.

Slap, A Gap, or narrow Pass between two Hills. *Slap,* a Breach in a Wall.

Slid, Smooth, cunning, slippery ; as, *He's a slid lown. Slidry,* Slippery.

Slonk, A Mire, Ditch or Slough.

Smirky, Smiling. [1800.]

Smoor, To smother.

Snack, Nimble, ready, clever.

Snell, Sharp, smarting, bitter, firm.

Snishing-mill, [Snuff-box].

Snod, Metaphorically used for Neat, Handsome, Tight.

Sonse, Sonsy, Happy, fortunate, lucky, sometimes used for large and lusty.

Sough, The Sound of Wind among the Trees, or of our Sleeping.

Souter, A shoemaker. [1800.]

Sowf, To conn over a Tune on an Instrument.

Spae, To foretel or divine. *Spaemen,* Prophets, Augurs.

Spang, A leap or Jump. To leap or jump.

Speel, To climb.

Speer, To ask, inquire.

Spence, The Place of the House where Provisions are kept.

Spunk-box, [Tinder-box].

Stang, Did sting ; also a Sting or Pole.

Starns, The Stars. *Starn*, a small Moity. We say, *Ne'er a Starn*.

Stend, or *Sten*. To move with a hasty long Pace.

Stent, To stretch or extend.

Stoup, A pot of tin of a certain measure. [1800.]

Stour, Dust agitated by Winds, Men or Horse Feet. *To Stour*, to run quickly.

Strath, A Plain on a River Side.

Streek, To stretch.

Sunkots, Something.

Swankies, Clever young Fellows.

Swats, Small Ale.

Sweer, Lazy, slow.

Swither, To be doubtful whether to do this or that, go this Way or the other.

Syne, Afterwards, then. [For *lang syne*, see *Sinsyne*.]

T

Taiken, Token. [1800.]

Tane, Taken.

Tappit hen, The *Scots* Quart, or *English* half Gallon Stoup.

Taz, A Whip or Scourge.

Ted, To scatter, spread ; as, *Tedding Hay*.

Tent, Attention. To observe. *Tenty*, headful, cautious.

Teugh, teughly, [Tough, toughly].

Theek, To thatch.

Thigg, To beg.

Thole, To endure, suffer.

Thowless, Unactive, silly, lazy, heavy.

Thrang, [*n*. Throng ; *adj*. Busy].

Thrawart, Forward, cross, crabbed.

Thrawn, Stern and Cross-grain'd.

Thrums, [A weaver].

Tift, Good Order, Health.

Till' t, To it. [1800]

Tine, tint, To lose. Lost.

Tip, Tippony, Ale sold for Two-pence the *Scots* Pint.

Tirle, To uncover a House, or undress a Person, strip one naked. Sometimes a short Action is named a *Tirle* ; as, *They took a Tirle of dancing, drinking, &c.*

Tod, A Fox.

Toolie, To fight. A Fight or Quarrel.

Toom, Empty, applied to a Barrel, Purse, House, &c. *Id.** To empty. [* 1728 *It.*]

Towmonds, A Year or Twelve-month.

Trig, Neat, handsome. [*Trigging*, adornment.]

Truff, Steal.

Twin, To part with, or separate from.

U

Umquhile, The late, or deceast sometime ago. Of old.

Unsenn, [Uninvited, unbidden].

W

Wair'd, [Spent, lavished].

Wakes, [Nocturnal expeditions].

Wald, [To wield, to manage].

Wale, To pick and chuse. *The Wale, i.e.* The best.

Wally, Chosen, beautiful, large. *A Bonny Wally, i.e.* A fine Thing. [Also, from *Wall*, wave, meaning tossing, weltering.]

Wame, Womb, [Stomach].

Wap, [Throw].

Wauking, [Walking.]
We'an, A Child.
Webster, [Weaver].
Weir, War.
Whilk, Which.
Whilliwaw, A Cheat.
Whinging, Whining, speaking with a doleful tone.
Whins, Furze.
Whist, Hush.   Hold your Peace.
Wid, *Wood*, Mad.
Wirrycow, A scarecrow or hob-goblin.

Wysing, Inclining.   *To wise*, To Lead, train ; as, *He's no sic a Gouk as to wise the Water by his ain Mill.*
Wyte, To blame.   Blame.

Y

Yesk, The Hickup.
Yet, Gate.
Yowff, A swinging Blow.
Yowk, [The yolk].

PRINTED IN GREAT BRITAIN BY OLIVER AND BOYD LTD., EDINBURGH